D0510188

about the **cross-eyed teacher**? Or the one about the **man who stole a lorry load of rhubarb**?

This tiny little book is **PACKED FULL** of *utterly bonkers jokes* and *riddles* to keep you laughing for hours.

Try them on your family and friends and give everyone a **chuckle**!

PUFFIN BOOKS

Published by the Penguin Group: London, New York,
Australia, Canada, India, Ireland, New Zealand and South Africa
Penguin Books Ltd, Registered Offices:
80 Strand, London WC2R 0RL, England

puffinbooks.com

First published 2013
001

Printed in Portugal by Printer Portuguesa

British Library Cataloguing in Publication Data
A CIP catalogue record for this book is available from the British Library

ISBN: 978-0-141-35231-2

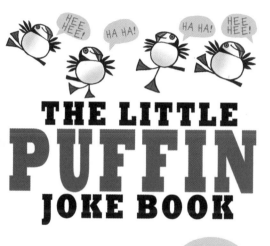

THE LITTLE
PUFFIN
JOKE BOOK

PUFFIN

Flick the book and see me move!

CONTENTS

Animal
Madness!

What do you
give a **sick bird**?

Tweetment.

Doctor, Doctor,
I keep thinking
I'm an owl.

Don't be
such a twit!

What's grey and white
and red all over?

**An embarrassed
elephant.**

What do you get if you cross
a fish with an elephant?

4

**Swimming
trunks.**

Why did the elephant
paint his toenails red?

**So he could hide in
the cherry tree!**

Where do horses go when they are sick?

Horsepital.

What did the horse say when he got to the bottom of his nosebag?

'This is the last straw!'

5

What do you call a donkey with three legs?

A wonkey.

Doctor, Doctor,
I think I'm a dog!

Take a seat!

I can't — I'm not
allowed on the furniture.

How do you
know when a dog's
been naughty?

**There's a little poodle
on the carpet ...**

What dog likes to have
a bubble-bath?
A shampoodle!

What's the
difference between
a **well-dressed man**
and a **tired dog**?

The man **wears a suit**,
the dog just **pants**.

What do you call
a cow eating grass?

A lawn-moo er.

What do you get when you
cross a cow with a duck?

**Cream
quackers.**

What do cows
like to dance to?

**Any kind of
moo sic you like!**

What do
hedgehogs eat for lunch?

Prickled onions.

10

What sound do porcupines
make when they kiss?

Ouch!

Doctor, Doctor, I've just swallowed a sheep!

How do you feel?

Very baa-aaa-d.

11

Two sheep were in a field.
'Baaa!' said one.
'I was going to say that!' said the other.

What do **apes cook**
their dinner on?

Gorillas.

Where do
baby gorillas sleep?
In apricots.

What do you call
a pig that can do karate?
A pork chop.

What do you call a pig with fleas? Pork scratching.

How do you fit more pigs on your farm? Build a sty-scraper!

What do you give a sick pig? OINKment!

How could you tell that the little seabird was out of breath?

It was a puffin.

Why does a penguin carry a fish in its beak?

Because it doesn't have any pockets!

What goes, 'Now you see me,

now you don't;

now you see me,

now you don't'?

A **penguin** on a **zebra crossing**.

What's a frog's favourite drink?
Croak-a cola!

What happens when a frog's car breaks down?

He gets **toad** away.

What kind of shoes do frogs like?

Open-toad sandals.

What do you call a bird that floats on the sea's surface?

Bob.

What fish sleeps underwater?

A kipper.

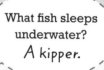

Why do fish live in salt water?

Because pepper makes them sneeze!

Doctor, Doctor,
I feel like a pony!

Don't worry, you're
just a little hoarse!

20

What did the horse
say when it fell over?

'I've fallen and I
can't **giddyup**!'

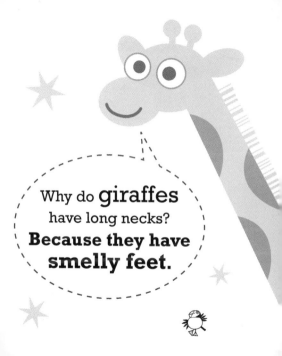

What did the farmer call the cow that had no milk?

An udder failure.

What happens if you walk under a cow?

I don't know. What does happen if you walk under a cow?

You get a pat on the head!

What do you get if you cross a
cement-mixer with a chicken?

A brick-layer.

Why does a
stork stand on
one leg?

Because it
would fall over
if it lifted the
other one.

What's a snake's favourite subject at school?

Hisssssstory.

Why is it hard to play cards in the jungle? **There are too many cheetahs!**

What does a puffin wear to the beach?

A beakini.

Why do **seagulls** fly over the sea?

Because if they flew over the bay they would be bagels!

Why are teddy
bears never hungry?
**Because they're
always stuffed!**

What's white, furry and shaped like a tooth?

A molar bear!

What do you call a camel with three humps?

Humphrey.

What do you get if you cross a dog with a hen?

Pooched eggs.

Excuse me, do you have any dogs going cheap?

I'm afraid not, they go woof-woof.

Do you know happened to the cat that swallowed a ball of wool?

She had mittens!

What is the largest mouse in the animal kingdom?

A hippopotamouse.

What do you get when you pour boiling water down a rabbit-hole?

A hot cross bunny.

What is a **penguin's** favourite **footwear**?

Flipper-floppers!

Funny Food!

Why did the jelly wobble?

Because it saw the milk shake.

Did you hear about the man who stole a lorry load of rhubarb?

He was put into custard-y!

Why are carrots good for your eyes?

Well, have you ever seen a rabbit with glasses?

What's the difference between an **elephant** and a **biscuit**?

You can't dunk an elephant in your tea.

Why did the banana
go to the doctor?

*Because he wasn't
peeling well.*

Why did the banana go
out with the prune?

**Because he couldn't
find a date.**

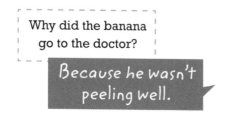

Waiter, do you have frog's legs?

No, sir, I just walk this way.

Doctor, Doctor, there's a strawberry stuck on my head!

Would you like some cream for it?

What do you call a
peanut in a spacesuit?

An astronut!

Why shouldn't
you tell a
joke to an
egg?

Because
it might
crack up!

Waiter, this food tastes kind of funny!

Then why aren't you laughing?

Why did the girl smear **peanut butter** on the road?

To go with the traffic jam!

Why did the
tomato blush?

**Because it
saw the salad
dressing!**

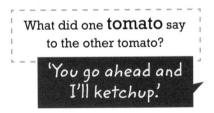

What did one **tomato** say
to the other tomato?

'You go ahead and
I'll ketchup.'

What do you get when you cross a **cheetah** and a **hamburger**?

Fast food!

What do you call **cheese** that isn't yours?

Nacho cheese!

What's a **penguin's** favourite salad?

Iceberg lettuce!

What do you give a sick lemon?

Lemon aid.

What is **square** and **green**?

A lemon in disguise.

What kind of shoes do you make out of banana skins?

Slippers.

What's **yellow** and **swings** from cake to cake?

Tarzipan!

What is bad-tempered
and goes with custard?
Apple grumble.

What's green and fluffy
and comes from Mars?
A Martian-mallow.

What's worse than finding a **maggot** in your **apple**?

Finding **half** a **maggot** in your **apple**!

Why can't you tell **secrets** on the **farm**?

Because the corn has ears and the potatoes have eyes.

What did one strawberry say to another strawberry?

'How did we get in this **jam**?'

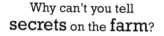

Waiter, will my pizza be long?

No, sir, it will be round!

How do you make a cream puff?

Chase it round the garden.

Where did the
spaghetti go to dance?

The meat ball.

53

Waiter: How did you find
your steak, madam?

I moved a lettuce leaf
and there it was!

What's the strongest
vegetable?

A muscle sprout.

54

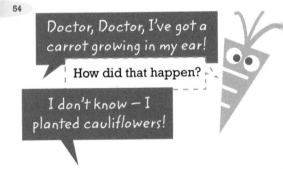

Doctor, Doctor, I've got a
carrot growing in my ear!

How did that happen?

I don't know — I
planted cauliflowers!

What's yellow on the outside and green in the middle?

A cucumber dressed as a banana.

What happened when someone trod on the grape?

It let out a little whine.

What do you call someone who peers through a **butcher's window**?

A mince spy.

How do you make a **sausage** roll?

Push it down a hill.

How can you tell if an **elephant's** been in your fridge?

There are footprints in the cheesecake.

What is the difference between a **piano** and a fish?

You can't **tuna** fish!

What is small, round
and giggles a lot?

A tickled onion.

What's the worst thing
about being an octopus?

**Washing your hands
before dinner!**

Why did the **baker** stop making **bagels**?

Because he was tired of the HOLE business.

What did one **plate** say to another?

'**Lunch is on me!**'

Silly
School!

Did you hear about the cross-eyed teacher?

He couldn't control his pupils!

Why is 6 afraid of 7?

Because 7 ate 9.

Why did the **nose** not want to go to **school**?

It was tired of getting picked on!

65

Who's the **king** of the pencil case?

The ruler.

How do **bees** get to school?

By school buzz!

What do **elves** learn in school?

The elf-abet!

What did the
pencil sharpener
say to the **pencil**?

**'Stop going in
circles
and get to
the point!'**

Why did the **jelly baby** go to school?

To become a Smartie!

Name three famous poles.

North, south and tad!

Why did the music teacher need a ladder?

To reach the high notes.

What did the calculator say to the other calculator?

'You can count on me!'

What do you get if you cross a **maths teacher** and a **clock**?

Arithma-ticks!

Which tables do you **not** have to learn?

Dinner tables.

Who designed Noah's ark?

An ark-itect!

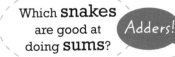

Which **snakes** are good at doing **sums**?

Adders!

72

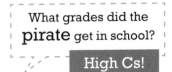

What grades did the **pirate** get in school?

High Cs!

Why did the student throw his **watch** out of the school window?

He wanted to see **time fly**.

Why is the school orchestra so smelly?

Because they have a large wind section.

What came after the Stone Age and the Bronze Age?

The sausage, sir!

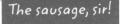

Why did the **maths** book look so sad?

Because it had a lot of **problems**.

What's the difference between a **teacher** and a **train**?

The teacher says, 'Spit out your gum,' and the train says, 'Chew, chew!'

What do elves do after school?

Gnome work.

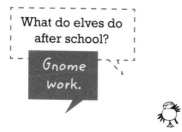

Why did the boy **eat** his homework?

Because the teacher said it was a piece of cake.

When is a blue book not a blue book?

When it is read!

What is

67 +

35 +

99 +

136 +

84?

A headache.

78

Why did the teacher turn the **lights** on?

Because her class was so dim.

What do you do if a teacher **rolls** her **eyes** at you?

Pick them up and roll them back!

What did you learn in school today, son?

Not enough, I have to go back tomorrow!

Billy, I think your dad has been helping you with your homework.

No, sir, he did it all himself.

I don't like my new **school** one bit. The teacher doesn't know a thing. All she does is ask **questions**!

Why are dinner ladies so **cruel**?

Because they batter fish, beat eggs and whip cream.

What is a **pirate's** favourite subject?

Arrrrrt!

I think my **teacher** really likes me.

She keeps putting kisses on my homework.

If I had six oranges in one hand and seven apples in the other, what would I have?

Very big hands!

If I cut two apples in half, four pears in quarters and added twelve grapes, what will I get?

Fruit salad.

What did the pen say to the pencil?

'What's your point?'

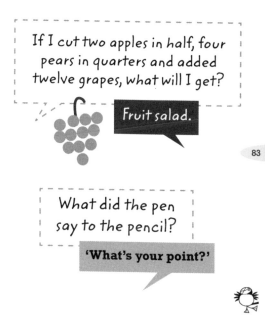

Teacher, Teacher, all the other kids keep calling me a werewolf!

Just ignore them, dear — now wipe your eyes and go and comb your face . . .

Why didn't the **zombie** go to school?

Because he was feeling **rotten**.

Utterly Bonkers!

What did one **eye** say to the other **eye**?

'There's something between us that smells.'

What did the **wig** say to the **head**?

'I've got you completely covered.'

There are
two eggs boiling in a pan.
One egg says to the other:
'It's very hot in here.'

The other says,
'Wait till you get outside.
They'll bash your
head in!'

Would you like a duck egg for tea, son?

Only if you quack it for me.

What did one toilet say to the other?

'You look a bit flushed.'

90

If **buttercups**
are yellow, what
colour are
hiccups?

Burple.

Why was the belt arrested?

Because it held up some pants!

Why do **vampires** brush their teeth?

To stop bat breath.

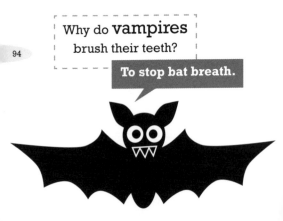

95

Why did the **man** with **one hand** cross the road?

To get to the second-hand shop.

What do you call a **woman** standing in the middle of a **tennis court**?

Annette!

What do you call a **man** lying on your **doorstep**?

Matt!

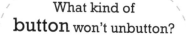

What kind of **button** won't unbutton?

A bellybutton!

What do **jelly babies** wear in the **rain**?

Gumboots.

What did **the astronaut** see in his frying pan?

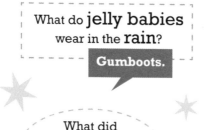

An unidentified frying object.

What's **mad** and goes to the **moon**?

A loony module.

Why did the **clown**
go to the doctor?

**Because he was
feeling a little funny!**

What did one
flag say to the other?

**Nothing, it
just waved!**

Why do birds fly south in winter?

Because it's too far to walk.

Why aren't elephants allowed on the beach?

Because they can't keep their trunks up.

I was once
in a play called
**'Breakfast in
Bed'**.

Did you
have a big
role?

No, just
toast and
marmalade!

Doctor, Doctor, I think I'm losing my memory.

When did it start?

When did what start?

What did the **hat** say to the **scarf**?

'You go on ahead and I'll hang around.'

What did the
father ghost say to the
naughty baby ghost?

**'Spook when
you're spooken to!'**

Doctor, doctor, I feel like everyone is ignoring me.

Next!

Why did
Mickey Mouse take
a trip into space?

**He wanted to
find Pluto!**

What goes 'ha-ha plonk'?

A skeleton laughing its head off.

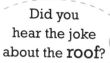

Did you hear the joke about the roof?

No.

Never mind, it's over your head!

What does a **cloud** wear under its **trousers**?

Thunder-pants!

What do you call a **skeleton** who won't work?

Lazy bones!

What do **zombies** like on their **chops**?

Grave-y.

What is an **insect's** favorite sport?

Cricket!

Doctor, Doctor, I keep thinking I'm a packet of biscuits.

What kinds of biscuits? Do you mean those square ones with lots of little holes in them?

Yes, that's right.

You're not mad — you're crackers!

Why did the **dog** cross the road?

Because it was doing an impression of a chicken.

What's a **twack**?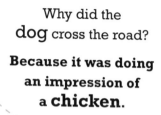

Something a twain runs on.

Why did **Tigger** look down the toilet?

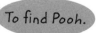 To find Pooh.

What did the hungry **Martian** say when it landed on **Earth**?

'Take me to your larder.'

What did the **policeman** say to his **tummy**?

'Don't move, I've got you under a vest!'

It all started with a Scarecrow . . .

Puffin is over **70** years old.

Sounds ancient, doesn't it?
But Puffin has never been so lively.

From the very first Puffin story book
about a man with broomstick arms called
Worzel Gummidge to **Matilda** and
Artemis Fowl, today there's a Puffin for
everyone. Whether it's a picture book or
a paperback, a sticker book or a joke book,
if it's got that little Puffin on it –
it's bound to be good.

BRIGHT AND SHINY AND SIZZLING WITH FUN STUFF ...

puffin.co.uk

WEB CHAT
Discover books, competitions and treats galore

WEB NEWS
Follow the Puffin Blog –
packed with posts from Puffin HQ

WEB FUN
Download activities, podcasts and more

WEBBED FEET
(Puffins have funny little feet
and brightly coloured beaks)